LODGE

COOKING

LET'S EAT !

Lodge Cooking
Michael R. Poll

A Cornerstone Book
Published by Cornerstone Book Publishers
An Imprint of Michael Poll Publishing
Copyright © 2016 by Michael R. Poll

Cornerstone Book Publishers
New Orleans, LA
www.cornerstonepublishers.com

First Cornerstone Edition - 2016

ISBN: 1-934935-04-2
ISBN-13:978-1-934935-04-0

MADE IN THE USA

Dedicated to the following ladies who helped make this book possible:
Eve Dawkins Poll; Eulalie Misenich; Vivian Ware; Alice Klebert; Edna Klebert;
Mary Ruth Wroten, Ruth Dawkins and Eulalie Eymas

Note: Serving Sizes are suggestions and are given as a general guide for
calculating the amount of ingredients that are needed in the recipes for
the number of guests at your meal.

Michael R. Poll

Lodge Cooking

Salads

Grand Master's Favorite
(Shrimp Remoulade)
Number of Servings: 4

INGREDIENTS
1 1/2 teaspoons salt
1/2 teaspoon white pepper
1/4 teaspoon cayenne pepper
2 tablespoons paprika
2 tablespoons finely chopped parsley
1 tablespoon finely minced garlic
1 1/2 teaspoons hot horseradish
2 tablespoons Creole mustard
2 tablespoons catsup
1 tablespoon Worcestershire sauce
2 tablespoons white vinegar
2 tablespoons lemon juice
4 tablespoons olive oil
2 ribs finely chopped celery
2 finely chopped shallots
1 pound peeled and deveined boiled shrimp

INSTRUCTIONS
In a blender combine all ingredients except shrimp, oil celery and shallots. Slowly add oil, blending thoroughly. Stir in celery and shallots. When well mixed pour into a bowl, cover and refrigerate overnight so flavors will blend. When ready to serve, place shrimp on a bed of shredded lettuce on individual salad plated. Spoon sauce over, covering the shrimp completely. Garnish each salad with hard-boiled egg and tomato wedges and black olives. Easily doubled for larger portions.

Master Mason Secret
(Apple-Celery Salad)
Number of servings: 6

INGREDIENTS
3 to 4 apples
2 stalks celery
1 cup pecans or walnuts
1/2 cup mayonnaise
Salt to taste

INSTRUCTIONS
Finely chop celery talks and put on the side. Chop the pecans and also put on the side. Peel the apples one at a time and chop into cubes. As you peel each apple quickly combine the cubes in a large bowl with the mayonnaise to prevent the apples from turning brown. Once all the apples are cubed and in the bowl then add the celery and pecans and thoroughly mix. More mayonnaise can be added if needed. Then salt the mixture to taste. Chill and then serve.

Quorum Tonight
(Shrimp Salad)
Number of servings: 6

INGREDIENTS
8 cups cooked, cleaned shrimp
2 cups chopped celery
2 cups chopped sweet pepper
2 tablespoons lemon juice
1 cup mayonnaise
1 teaspoon salt
1/8 teaspoon cayenne pepper (or to taste)

INSTRUCTIONS
Blend mayonnaise, lemon juice, salt, and pepper in a bowl. Add shrimp, celery and sweet pepper and toss lightly. Serve on lettuce and tomato lined plate. Can be garnished with hard cooked egg and olives.

Craft Feast
(Potato Salad)
Number of servings: 8

INGREDIENTS

4 pounds potatoes (preferably small red)
1 large onion, finely chopped
4 stalks celery, finely chopped
1/2 sweet pepper, finely chopped
6 scallions (green onions), finely chopped
6 hard boiled eggs, chopped
1/2 medium size jar of olives and pimentos, sliced
3/4 cup mayonnaise
1/4 cup yellow mustard
2 tablespoons white vinegar
Salt and black pepper to taste

INSTRUCTIONS

Mix the mayonnaise and mustard and place on the side. Boil the potatoes for about 20 to 25 minutes or until soft (not falling apart). Drain and cool until handled easily. Peel and cut into 1/4 inch slices. Place potatoes in a large bowl. Mix in onions, celery, olives, scallions, and gently add hard boiled eggs. Add the vinegar and mayo-mustard mix. Salt and pepper to taste.

Hiram's Salad
(Chicken, Rice and Artichoke Salad)
Number of servings: 4

INGREDIENTS
2 cups uncooked rice
2 cups chicken broth
2 teaspoons lemon juice
1/2 teaspoon rosemary
1 bay leaf
1 1/2 cups cooked chicken chunks
1 jar undrained marinated artichoke hearts
1/2 cup chopped pecans or walnuts
1/3 cup sweet pepper strips
1/3 cup shredded carrots

INSTRUCTIONS
Add chicken broth, lemon juice, rosemary, and bay leaf to uncooked rice. Mix well and steam until tender. Remove bay leaf and cool rice thoroughly. Combine rest of ingredients, add rice and toss.

Labor to Refreshment
(Seven Fruit Salad)
Number of servings: 6

INGREDIENTS
1 cup fresh pineapple chunks or 6 ounce can pineapple chucks, drained
1 cup fresh sliced peaches, 1 cup frozen sliced peaches, or 18 ounce can sliced peaches, drained
1/4 cantaloupe, peeled and cut into wedges
1/2 cup seedless grapes, halved
1/2 cup fresh strawberries, halved
1/4 honeydew melon or water melon, cut into balls
1 large or 2 small oranges, peeled and sectioned
Halved pecans (optional)

INSTRUCTIONS
Line bowl with lettuce. Mix and toss fruit gently and arrange in bowl. Serve with lemon honey dressing separately.

Soups

Clean Apron
(Artichoke and Oyster Soup)
Number of servings: 6

INGREDIENTS
1 can (14 ounces) Artichoke hearts, drained and chopped well
2 dozens oysters and oyster water
2 bunch shallots, chopped fine
2 ribs celery, chopped fine
6 tablespoons butter
2 tablespoons flour
2 cups water
1 teaspoon salt
1/2 teaspoon black pepper
1/4 teaspoon thyme
2 bay leaves
1 can chicken broth

INSTRUCTIONS
Poach oysters in oyster water until edges curl. Set aside. Meanwhile sauté shallots and celery in butter until tender. With pot over low heat, add flour, stirring constantly for a few minutes. Add the water, oysters, oyster water, artichokes, salt, pepper, thyme, chicken broth, and bay leaves. Bring to boil and immediately lower to simmer. Cook for about 20 minutes. Remove bay leaves and serve immediately.

Tyler's Special
(Vegetable Soup)
Number of servings: 12

INGREDIENTS
6 pounds beef brisket or chuck roast
6 sprigs parsley, chopped
3 large Creole tomatoes, chopped
1 can small peas, drained
4 large carrots, sliced
1 small bag frozen corn
2 large white onions, chopped
2 tablespoons slat
3 ribs celery, chopped
1 teaspoon black pepper
1/3 cup celery leaves, chopped
1 teaspoon thyme
3 small turnips, chopped
1/2 teaspoon garlic powder
1/2 small cabbage, shredded
1/4 teaspoon cayenne pepper
1/2 pound snap beans, quartered
2 potatoes, chopped
3 bay leaves
1 tablespoon Worchestershire sauce
Vermicelli
About 6 quarts water

INSTRUCTIONS

In a large (about 10 quarts) soup pot put all ingredients except seasonings and vermicelli. Add water, enough to cover generously, and bring to a boil. Lower heat to simmer, keep pot partially covered. After pot has been simmering for about 10 minutes, skim top of soup and then add seasonings. Continue for 4 to 5 hours. Vermicelli may be added to soup during the last 20 minutes of cooking. When soup is done, remove meat. Cut off about two thirds of the meat and set it aside. Cut remaining meat into small pieces and return to soup.

Variation: Steam or boil 6 large, peeled, whole white potatoes. After serving soup as a first course, slice meat that was set aside and serve, along with a large sliced red onion and the steamed potatoes, as an entrée with horseradish sauce.

Square Enjoyment
(Seafood Gumbo)
Number of servings: 8

INGREDIENTS
2 pounds. large shrimp, peeled and drained*
1 pound fresh or frozen crab
1 quart oyster and oyster water
1/2 pound slice raw ham, cut into cubes
2/3 cup bacon drippings or oil
2/3 cup flour
2 onions, chopped
4 cloves garlic, minced
1 large sweet pepper, chopped
2 ribs celery, chopped
1/3 cup parsley, chopped fine
1/2 cup shallots, chopped
2 bay leaves
4 teaspoons salt
1 teaspoon black pepper
1/4 teaspoon cayenne
1 teaspoon thyme
1 tablespoon Worcestershire
2 quarts hot water
3 tablespoons filed powder
Steamed rice

INSTRUCTIONS
In a large pot (preferably iron) make a roux by gradually adding flour to the oil, stirring constantly over low heat. When it is dark brown, quickly add ham, onion, sweet pepper, shallots, celery, parsley, and garlic. Cook over low heat about 10 minutes more, stirring constantly. Then add one half cup of the water and the rest of the seasonings except the file. Still keeping a very low heat, gradually add the rest of the water. Raise heat, and bring to a quick boil, continuing to stir. Again reduce heat to low and cook for about 20 minutes. Add shrimp and crabmeat and simmer for 20 minutes more, adding oysters and oyster water after 15 minutes. Remove pot from heat and let simmering stop. Add file and stir. Let it sit for about 5 minutes. Serve over deep bowls of steaming rice.

Warm Fellowship
(Busy-Day Soup)
Number of servings: 6

INGREDIENTS
1 (10 1/2 ounce) can green pea soup
2 (10 1/2 ounce) cans tomato soup
2 (10 1/2 ounce) cans cream of mushroom soup
2 cups milk
3/4 cup water
1 1/4 cup dry sherry or sauterne wine
1 pound crabmeat, drained

INSTRUCTIONS
In a large saucepan, mix soups, milk, water, and wine. Cook, stirring well, until blended. Stir in crabmeat and heat well. May be refrigerated up to 2 days.

Level Bowl
(Broccoli Soup)
Number of servings: 4 - 6

INGREDIENTS
1 small onion
1 or 2 ribs celery
1 carrot
2 tablespoons butter or margarine
3 large stalks of broccoli
3 cups chicken broth
1 1/2 cups yogurt
Salt & Pepper

INSTRUCTIONS
Chop the onion, celery, and carrot. In large pan sauté them in butter for about 5 minutes on medium heat or until soft. Stir continually. Wash the broccoli, cutting off the buds. Place the buds on the side. Peel the stalks and coarsely chop them. Put the chopped broccoli stalks in the pan* with the sautéed vegetables. Add chicken broth and bring to a boil. Reduce the heat and simmer for 15 minutes. Add the buds and cook for 5 minutes more. Puree the soup in a blender, about 2 cups at a time. Add yogurt then season with salt and pepper to taste.

Secretary's Cure
(Chicken Soup)
Number of servings: 8 - 12

INGREDIENTS
1 large chicken, cut up
3 celery ribs, chopped
2 medium onions, chopped fine
3 cloves garlic, minced
2 bay leaves
1/3 cup chopped parsley
1 tablespoon crushed thyme
1 tablespoon salt
1/2 teaspoon pepper
1/2 cup pearl barley (optional)
1 cup sauterne wine (optional)
6 quarts water (about)
Egg noodles

INSTRUCTIONS
Combine all ingredients except egg noodles in a large soup pot. Bring to a boil, lower heat to simmer, and simmer for 4 ½ to 5 hours. Remove chicken and add egg noodles to broth, cooing until noodles are tender. Meanwhile remove chicken from bones, cut into bite size pieces, and add to pot. Stir and serve.

Steps to Enjoyment
(Chicken and Sausage Gumbo
with Microwaved Roux)
Number of Servings: 8 to 12

Prepared microwave roux with vegetables (see below)
1 pound Andouille sausage or polish Kielbasa sausage, thinly sliced or diced
Chicken stock or chicken stock and hot water to equal 3 quarts
1 (5 pound) "cooked" chicken, (see below) boned and cut in bite size pieces
1 tablespoon salt
1/2 teaspoon black pepper
1/4 teaspoon cayenne pepper (or to taste)
1 bay leaf
2 teaspoons crushed thyme
1 tablespoon basil

Microwaves Roux: This amount of roux will thicken 3 quarts of liquid to a gumbo consistency

1 cup oil
1 cup flour
2 cups chopped onions
2 cups chopped celery
1 cup chopped green pepper
2 cups shallots (green onions)
1/4 cup chopped garlic
1/2 cup chopped parsley

Mix oil and flour together in a large (6 cup) microwave safe measuring cup or bowl. Microwave uncovered on high for 7 to 10 minutes. Stir and continue to cook, stirring about every 30 seconds to a minute, until roux reaches a very dark caramel color. The right shade should take about 15 to 18 minutes total. (Be sure you do not let the roux burn.) Carefully remove the hot roux from the microwave and stir onion, celery, green onions, and sweet pepper into roux, making sure you stir well, bringing the roux up from the bottom of bowl or measuring cup. Return to microwave and cook for 4 minutes. Remove roux again from microwave and stir in the garlic and parsley. Cook on high for 2 minutes.

Chicken Cooked in Microwave

INGREDIENTS
2 to 3 pound chicken, cut up
1/2 onion, sliced
1 rib celery and leaves, cut into pieces
1 1/2 teaspoons salt
1/2 teaspoon cayenne pepper
1/2 cup dry Vermouth or Satuerne wine
2 cups hot water

INSTRUCTIONS
Place chicken and rest of ingredients in a large, covered, microwave safe, three to five quart casserole. Cook on high for 25 minutes. After cooked, marinate in stock in refrigerator until cool, or overnight. Remove chicken, strain and discard vegetables, and reserve stock. Bone chicken and cut into bite size pieces. Both chicken and stock can be frozen for future use and used for Jambalaya, Gumbo, or any recipe calling for cooked chicken.

Gumbo:

Remove roux mixture from microwave and pour into a large heavy pot (not iron) over medium heat. Add sausage and chicken to roux mixture. Lower heat and sauté about 6-7 minutes, stirring constantly. Slowly add chicken stock, okra if using, and seasonings, stirring well. Bring to a full boil, stir well, then lower heat to a simmer. Cook, partially covered, for about 45 minutes to an hour, stirring occasionally. Serve over steamed or boiled rice.

Sides

High Twelve Pasta
(Cauliflower and Spaghetti)
Number of servings: 6 - 8

INGREDIENTS
1 head of cauliflower
8 ounce package of spaghetti (vermicelli or extra thin spaghetti)
1/4 to 1/3 cup extra virgin olive oil
1/4 cup of parmesan cheese
1 teaspoon of garlic powder
1 teaspoon of Cajun spice
Salt to taste

INSTRUCTIONS
Clean cauliflower breaking into small pieces, or cauliflowerets. Add cauliflowerets to a pot of boiling water with 1/2 teaspoon salt and dash of olive oil. Cook about 8 minutes, then remove from water and drain. Cook spaghetti in same water about 8 minutes. Don't overcook!!! Put cauliflowerets in a large dish and add the olive oil, garlic powder, Cajun spice and a little salt. Add cooked spaghetti and mix.

Candidate's Preference
(Stuffed Tomatoes)
Number of servings: 8

INGREDIENTS
8 medium size tomatoes
1 egg, beaten
1 scallion top (green onion), finely chopped
2 tablespoons butter or margarine
1 cup ground ham or ground beef
Bread crumbs
2 cups stale bread, softened in milk
1 teaspoon Cajun spice
1 teaspoon salt
1/4 teaspoon pepper

INSTRUCTIONS
Cut hole in top of tomatoes and scoop out inside pulp, turning upside down to drain. Sauté onion to light brown in butter, adding pulp and ham or ground beef. Cook until nearly all liquid is out of tomatoes. Squeeze out all excess milk in bread, measuring 1 1/2 cups of the bread. Add this to ham mixture, also adding the egg, Cajun spice, salt and pepper. Mix well, then stuffing the tomato shells with this dressing and sprinkling the top with bread crumbs. Bake at 350 degrees for about 15 minutes.

24

Between the Compasses
(Vegetables and Rice)
Number of servings: 6

INGREDIENTS
2 cups of cooked rice
1 small onion, chopped
1 clove garlic, minced
1 pack frozen broccoli florets
1 (16 ounce) can tomatoes, drained and chopped
1/2 teaspoon salt
1/4 teaspoon pepper
1/4 teaspoon oregano
2 tablespoons butter or margarine

INSTRUCTIONS
Sauté chopped onion, garlic and broccoli in margarine until soft. Add rice, corn and tomatoes. Season with salt, pepper and oregano and mix well. Cover and simmer for about 15 minutes.

Save for the Master
(Black-eyed Pea Jambalaya)
Number of servings: 8 - 12

INGREDIENTS
2 pounds dried black-eyed peas, sorted and washed
1 ham hock or one cup chopped baked ham
1/2 pound Kielbasa sausage sliced
9 cups hot water
1/2 cup Sauterne or dry vermouth wine (optional)
1 large onion, chopped
2 cloves garlic, minced
1/2 cup chopped parsley
1 can (28 ounce) tomatoes, undrained and chopped
1/4 teaspoon cayenne pepper (or to taste)
1 tablespoon Worcestershire sauce
4 chicken boullion cubes
2 teaspoon salt (or to taste)
1/4 teaspoon oregano
1/4 teaspoon thyme
2 bay leaves
2 1/2 cups raw rice

INSTRUCTIONS
Presoak beans. Drain peas then add peas and rest of ingredients except rice to a large pot. Bring to a boil and immediately lower heat and simmer for about 2 hours. If using ham hock remove ham hock and cut meat from bone. Return meat to pot along with rice. Cover and simmer for about 20 minutes or until rice and peas are tender. Remove and discard bay leaves.

Hiram's Jewel
(Fried Eggplant)
Number of servings: 6

INGREDIENTS
1 large eggplant, cut into thin slices
1 egg, beaten with 1/2 tablespoon water
1/2 teaspoon pepper
1 teaspoon salt
1 cup Progresso seasoned breadcrumbs
6 tablespoons grated parmesan cheese
Hot oil

INSTRUCTIONS
Combine egg and water and beat well, in another bowl mix the bread crumbs, salt, pepper and parmesan cheese. Dip eggplant first in egg and then into crumbs and cheese. Coat well on both sides. Place on wax paper for about 10 minutes Fry in hot oil until golden. Drain on paper towels.

Under the Rods Peppers
(Stuffed Sweet Peppers)
Number of servings: 4

INGREDIENTS
4 large sweet peppers
1 pound raw shrimp, cleaned and chopped
1/2 pound sliced raw ham, chopped
1/4 cup bacon drippings
1 large onion, chopped
3 cloves garlic, minced
1 sweet pepper, chopped
1 rib celery
3/4 teaspoon salt
1/4 teaspoon black pepper
1/8 teaspoon (or more) -cayenne pepper
1 tablespoon chopped parsley
1 bay leaf
1 egg, beaten
1 cup bread crust, soaked in water and squeezed dry
Italian cheese and butter

INSTRUCTIONS
Cut off the top fourth of the sweet peppers and remove the seeds and membranes. Place the peppers upright in 1/2 inch salted water in a pot. Bring water to boil, cover, lower flame and cook for 5 minutes. Remove peppers, drain and set aside. Lightly brown onions, garlic, chopped sweet pepper, shrimp and ham in bacon drippings. Add bread and seasonings. Mix well and cook a few minutes longer. Remove from heat, and add egg. Cook one minute longer, stirring well. Stuff peppers. Sprinkle dry bread crumbs and Italian cheese on top. Put a little butter on each pepper. Bake at 375 degrees in a preheated oven for 35 to 40 minutes, or until tender and brown on top. Recipe easily doubled.

Five Points Potatoes
(Fried Sweet Potatoes)
Number of servings: 6

INGREDIENTS
4 medium sweet potatoes or yams
3 tablespoons butter
2 tablespoons oil
Salt and pepper to taste

INSTRUCTIONS
Boil or steam potatoes until fork tender. Remove skins and cut in slices 1/4 inch thick. Fry in butter and oil until brown. Sprinkle lightly with salt and pepper. Goes well with baked ham or pork chops.

Entrees

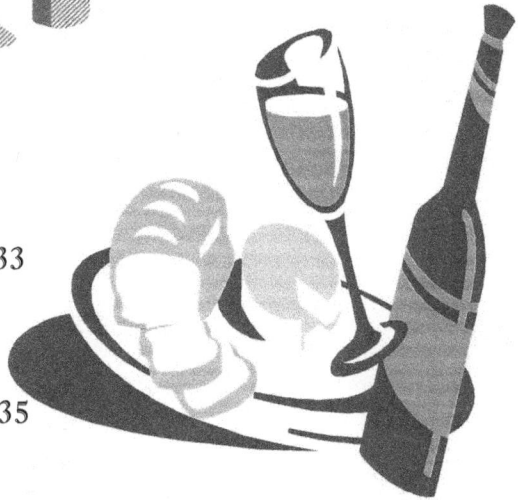

Master's Appreciation Feast
(Chicken and Wine)
Number of servings: 8

INGREDIENTS
2 broilers (young chickens) each cut in fourths
Salt, pepper, paprika and garlic powder
1/2 cup melted butter or margarine
1 large can sliced mushrooms
3 tablespoons chopped parsley
Juice of 1 lemon
1 cup sauterne or vermouth wine

INSTRUCTIONS
Sprinkle chicken generously with salt, pepper, paprika and garlic powder. Put in baking pan skin down. Pour melted butter and wine over chicken. Cover pan with plastic wrap and marinate in refrigerator several hours, or preferably overnight. When ready to bake, remove saran wrap and place in a 375 degree preheated oven for 30 minutes. After baking 30 minutes, turn chicken skin side up and bake an additional 30 minutes, basting occasionally. Goes well with buttered egg noodles or baked potato.

Clear Ballot Delight
(Catfish Etoufee)
Number of servings: 6 - 8

INGREDIENTS
5 pounds catfish, cut in large pieces
1/4 cup water
1 teaspoon salt
1 teaspoon black pepper
1/4 teaspoon Cajun spice
3 tablespoons salad oil
2 cloves garlic, minced
1 cup parsley, chopped
1 large bell pepper , finely chopped
1 large bay leaf
2 tablespoons flour
1/4 teaspoon thyme
3 stalks celery, finely chopped
2 slices lemon
1 cup green onions (white and green parts), finely chopped
1 1/2 cans tomato sauce

INSTRUCTIONS
Select a large pot that you can handle well enough to shake, as you never stir the fish while it is cooking. Season the pieces of fish well with a mixture of the salt, black pepper, and Cajun spice. Put oil in the unheated pot. Arrange half of the fish on the bottom. Mix the chopped vegetables and sprinkle half over fish. Sprinkle 1 tablespoon flour over the vegetables and half of the tomato sauce and then repeat. Add the thyme, bay leaf, lemon and 1/4 cup water. Place pot over low flame and cook slowly for one hour or until fish is tender. Shake pot often to keep from sticking. Never stir as this will break the fish. When tender, taste for seasoning and add more if necessary. Can serve as is or over steamed rice.

Warden's Favorite
(Broiled Fish Fillets)
Number of servings: 4 - 6

INGREDIENTS
6 to 8 medium sized filets (Can use trout, catfish, flounder or similar fish)
Salt to taste
Cajun spice and black pepper to taste
1 stick butter or margarine
2 teaspoons Worcestershire sauce
2 teaspoons lemon juice
Chopped parsley
Lemon slices

INSTRUCTIONS
Place filets on aluminum foil in shallow pan, season generously with salt, Cajun spice, and black pepper. Melt butter in small pan, adding Worcestershire sauce and lemon juice. Pour melted butter over filets and broil in preheated oven from 10 to 12 minutes, until nicely browned, without turning. Garnish with chopped parsley and lemon juice.

District Deputy's Visit
(Paneed Veal)
Number of servings: 4

INGREDIENTS
2 pounds veal rounds
2 eggs, and 3 tablespoons milk, beaten well
3 teaspoons salt
1/2 teaspoon black pepper
2 tablespoons paprika
1/2 teaspoon garlic powder
1 cup Italian bread crumbs

INSTRUCTIONS
Cut veal rounds into 4 pieces each. Pound with mallet until thin and tender. Combine salt, pepper, paprika, garlic, and bread crumbs. Dip meat into egg and milk mixture, then into bread crumb mixture. Refrigerate in single layer for about an hour or until dry. In heavy pan heat about 2 inches of oil until very hot. Fry meat until brown on both sides. Drain on paper towels. If you would like it extra crispy, coat first with flour, then egg and brad crumbs as above.

Northeast Corner Repast
(Oyster Loaf)
Number of servings: 2 - 3

INGREDIENTS
1 loaf unsliced French bread
1 dozen large oysters
1 cup bread crumbs
1 egg
1/2 cup cream
1 cup cooking oil
Dill pickles
Lemon
Ketchup
Butter
Salt and black pepper, and cayenne pepper to taste

INSTRUCTIONS
Slicing French bread in half, toast both halves. Butter insider and keep warm. Towel dry oysters. Mixing the egg with salt, black pepper, and cayenne pepper slowly add the cream. Dip the oysters in egg mixture and then bread crumbs. Fry in oil until brown and then drain. Fill the hollow of French bread loaf with the fried oysters. Garnish with sliced dill pickles, lemon and Ketchup. Replace top, heat in oven and serve.

Election Surprise
(Rice Sabrosa)
Number of servings: 6 - 8

INGREDIENTS
1 pound lean ground beef or turkey
1 large chopped onion
1 large chopped sweet pepper
2 teaspoons garlic puree or 2 garlic cloves, minced
1 tablespoon chili powder
2 teaspoons black pepper
2 cups (16 ounces.) canned tomatoes, chopped
3 cups cooked rice
1 cup grated cheddar cheese

INSTRUCTIONS
In a large skillet sauté beef, onions, and sweet peppers with seasonings until meat is lightly browned and vegetables are tender, stirring frequently to crumble meat. Add tomatoes and rice, mixing well. Pour into oven proof casserole. Top with cheese and put into preheated 350 degree oven until cheese melts. Recipe easily doubled.

Degree Night Spread
(Chicken Stew)
Number of servings: 4 - 6

INGREDIENTS
1 whole chicken (about 6 pounds) cut up to fry
1 cup milk
1/2 cup flour
1 stick margarine or butter
1 onion, finely chopped
2 stalks celery, finely chopped
1 green bell pepper, finely chopped
4 cloves garlic, finely chopped
1 tablespoon Worcestershire sauce
Cajun spice or salt, black pepper, and cayenne to taste

INSTRUCTIONS
Season chicken thoroughly with Cajun spice or salt, black pepper, and cayenne pepper. Melt margarine or butter in Dutch oven over a medium heat. Dip chicken in milk, then flour, and fry in margarine or butter until brown. Remove chicken.

Saute onion, celery, bell pepper, and garlic over a medium heat until tender. Add chicken and enough water to cover. Add Worcestershire sauce, cover partially, and cook slowly over a low heat until tender. Takes about 4 hours. Serve with rice or spaghetti.

Trestleboard Dinner
(String beans and Ham)
Number of servings: 4 - 6

INGREDIENTS
2 pounds string (green) beans or
2 large cans cut green beans
1 pound ham pieces, cut into small cubes
2 tablespoons oil
2 tablespoons butter
1 tablespoon flour
1 large onion, chopped
2 cloves garlic, minced
Salt to taste (add at end of cooking time)
1 teaspoon black pepper
1/2 teaspoon thyme
4 medium potatoes, peeled and cut into pieces
1 tablespoon Worcestershire sauce
4 cups hot water

INSTRUCTIONS
Snap ends off beans, break into fourths. Wash and set aside. Melt butter with oil in pan. Add flour and stir until smooth. Add onion and garlic and sauté until soft. Add ham, stir, and then beans, water and seasonings. Cooks about one hour or until beans are tender and potatoes are soft. Add salt to taste. Good served with crisy French bread or corn bread.

Meeting Incentive
(Lagniappe Casserole)
Number of servings: 8 - 10

INGREDIENTS

This casserole can be made with almost anything. We use it with 1 large can tuna or 1 large can of salmon, or a combination of a small can of each, 8 hot dogs, cut up, or a small ham steak, cubed.

Choice of the above
4 cups elbow macaroni
1 can cheddar cheese soup
1 can celery or mushroom soup
2 1/2 cans milk (3cups)
1 teaspoon salt
1/4 teaspoon black pepper
1/2 teaspoon dry mustard
1 teaspoon paprika'1/4 teaspoon thyme
Dash of cayenne pepper
1 tablespoon parsley
1 tablespoon Worcestershire sauce
1 small sweet pepper, chopped
1 small jar stuffed olives, halved (optional)
Seasoned bread crumbs and paprika

INSTRUCTIONS

Preheat oven to 350 degrees. Boil macaroni in salted water. Meanwhile in a saucepan heat soups, add Worcestershire sauce, milk, and seasonings. Bring to simmer, add sweet pepper and your choice of tuna, etc. and olives. Mix well. Put drained macaroni in large oblong or rectangular oven proof casserole. Pour sauce over macaroni. Mix well. Sprinkle bread crumbs liberally over top. Sprinkle with paprika and dot with butter. Bake at 350 degrees for 30 minutes.

Tip the Master's Hat
(Barbecue Shrimp)
Number of servings: 6

INGREDIENTS
1 1/2 to 2 pounds headless, medium to large shrimp
1 stick butter or margarine
1/2 cup Italian dressing
1 tablespoon Cajun spice
1 tablespoon garlic powder
2 tablespoons Worcestershire sauce
Salt to taste

INSTRUCTIONS
Wash shrimp well and spread out in a shallow pan. Combine butter, Italian dressing, Cajun seasoning, garlic powder, Worcestershire, and salt in a saucepan and heat over low heat. Let simmer for ten minutes then pour over shrimp. Mix well and refrigerate for 1 to 2 hours. Preheat oven to 300 degrees. Bake shrimp mixture for 30 minutes, turning every ten minutes. Serve with French bread to dip in sauce.

Fir for Solomon
(Beef Stew)
Number of servings: 6

INGREDIENTS
2 pounds boneless beef stew meat
1/3 cup vegetable oil
1/4 cup flour
1 large onion, chopped
4 cloves garlic, minced
1 large. sweet pepper
1 large can whole tomatoes
1 tablespoon salt
1/2 teaspoon black pepper
1/2 teaspoon thyme leaves
1/8 teaspoon cayenne pepper
1/2 cup chopped parsley
2 tablespoons Worcestershire sauce
1 can petit pois peas
1 large can sliced mushrooms
5 cups boiling water
2 stalks celery, cut in pieces of 1 ½ inch
4 carrots, halved lengthwise and cut into pieces
4 potatoes, peeled and cut in eight pieces

INTRUCTIONS
Put flour in a bowl or plastic bag. Drop in meat, a few pieces at a time and toss until well coated. Reserve leftover flour. Slowly brown meat in hot oil in heavy pot, a few pieces at a time. Remove pieces as they brown. Add onions, garlic, and sweet pepper to pot and sauté until just tender. Add tomatoes, salt, pepper, cayenne pepper, thyme, parsley and Worcestershire sauce. Simmer, stirring until well blended. Add boiling water, stir and then add meat, and rest of vegetables. Stir and simmer, covered, over low heat about 2 1/2 hours, or until meat is fork tender.

Variation: 1 cup of red wine may be substituted for one cup of water.

Third Degree Feast
(Chicken and Sausage Jambalaya L'Acadien)
Number of servings: 8

As in the preparation of gumbo, chop the vegetables, measure out the seasonings, and cut up the main ingredients before beginning to cook. If you do not have frozen chicken and stock available, prepare chicken according to "Cooked chicken" recipe the day before cooking Jambalaya. Marinate overnight.

INGREDIENTS
1 chicken, cut up and cooked (Can use recipe for Microwave chicken)
2 tablespoons cooking oil
1 pound Andouille sausage or Polish Kielbasa sausage, sliced thin
1/2 pound baked ham, cubes small (optional)
2 medium or 1 very large onion, chopped
3/4 cup thinly sliced green shallot (scallion) tops
4 cloves garlic, minced
1 large sweet pepper, chopped
2 ribs celery, chopped
3 tablespoons finely chopped parsley
3 1/2 teaspoon salt (or to taste)
1 teaspoon black pepper
1/4 teaspoon Cayenne pepper (or to taste)
1/2 teaspoon chili powder
1 teaspoon paprika
2 bay leaves, broken in half
1/2 teaspoon dried thyme leaves
1/4 teaspoon basil
1 tablespoon Worcestershire sauce
6 cups chicken stock, or chicken stock with water added to equal 6 cups

INSTRUCTIONS

In large heavy pot heat oil over high heat. Add sausage and vegetables to pot and reduce heat to medium. If you are including ham, add at this time. Cook, stirring frequently until slightly brown, about 10 minutes. Add seasonings, Worcestershire sauce and chicken. Stir well and then add chicken stock and rice. Stir gently, raise the heat to high and bring to a boil. Then turn the heat very low, stir and cover the pot. Cook for about 45 minutes, uncovering from time to time to stir. Remove the cover for the last 10 minutes or so and raise the heat to medium. Stir gently as the rice dries out, checking to make sure the mixture does not stick on the bottom or dry out too much. Serve immediately.

Variation: To make Creole Jambalaya, add 1 large can Italian tomatoes (28 ounce) chopped, along with chicken stock and rice. (Creole Jambalaya is with tomatoes added, Cajun Jambalaya does not use tomatoes.) Jambalaya freezes well.

Chicken Cooked in Microwave

INGREDIENTS
2 to 3 pound chicken, cut up
1/2 onion, sliced
1 rib celery and leaves, cut into pieces
1 1/2 teaspoons salt
1/2 teaspoon cayenne pepper
1/2 cup dry Vermouth or Satuerne wine
2 cups hot water

INSTRUCTIONS

Place chicken and rest of ingredients in a large, covered, microwave safe, three to five quart casserole. Cook on high for 25 minutes. After cooked, marinate in stock in refrigerator until cool, or overnight. Remove chicken, strain and discard vegetables, and reserve stock. Bone chicken and cut into bite size pieces. Both chicken and stock can be frozen for future use and used for Jambalaya, Gumbo, or any recipe calling for cooked chicken.

Spice up the Ceremonies
(Meat Loaf and Brown Gravy)
Number of Servings 8 - 10

INGREDIENTS
2 pounds ground beef or 1 1/2 pounds ground beef and 1/2 pounds ground pork
1 large onion. Chopped
2 cloves garlic, minced
1 sweet pepper, chopped
2 eggs, slightly beaten
1 cup seasoned bread crumbs
1 cup uncooked oatmeal
2 tablespoons Worcestershire
3/4 cup milk or red wine
1 1/2 teaspoon salt
1/2 teaspoon pepper
1/8 teaspoon cayenne pepper
2 tablespoons parsley
2 tablespoons Parmesan cheese

Brown Gravy
Bacon drippings plus oil from pan to equal 1/3 cup
1/3 cup flour
Salt, pepper, garlic salt to taste
1 tablespoon kitchen bouquet
1 can drained sliced mushrooms (optional)
3 cups boiling water

INSTRUCTIONS
Preheat oven to 350 degrees. In large bowl, mix all ingredients together thoroughly. Shape into two loaves. Both can be cooked at once or freeze one for another time. Place in open shallow baking pan to which 1/4 cup bacon drippings have been added. Bake for 45 minutes to one hour. Remove from pan an dlet meat loaf sit for about 15 minutes while you make brown gravy from the pan drippings.

Make gravy. When browned, slowly add water and seasonings. Add mushrooms. Stir slowly and simmer about 10 to 15 minutes. Serve with meat loaf and either steamed rice or egg noodles.

Regular Masonic Feast
(Red Beans and Rice)
Number of servings: 6 - 8

INGREDIENTS
1 pound dried red beans or 5 cans red beans
1 pound pickle pork or 1 pound ham seasoned
1 large onion, chopped fine
3 cloves garlic, minced
1 sweet pepper, chopped fine
2 tablespoons parsley, chopped fine
1 1/2 teaspoon salt (added after beans are cooked)
1/2 teaspoon black pepper
1/8 teaspoon cayenne pepper
1/2 teaspoon thyme
2 bay leaves
1 tablespoon Worcestershire sauce
½ cup dry red wine (optional)
About 3 cups water
Steamed rice

INSTRUCTIONS
Add dried or canned red beans to a large iron or heavy pot. If using canned beans, rinse cans with water and add to pot. If using dried beans add soaking water to equal to 3 or 4 cups along with all other ingredients except rice. Bring to a boil, stir well, then lower heat. Cover and simmer for about 2 to 3 hours, or until beans are tender and gravy has thickened. Mash some beans against the side of the pot with spoon to make the gravy richer and thicker. Add more water if needed. Stir often during the cooking to make sure the beans do not stick to the pot. When the beans are cooked, add salt and serve with steamed rice. If any are left over, beans freeze very well. Recipe is easily doubled.

Passing the Ritual
(Chili)
Number of servings: 8

INGREDIENTS
1 1/2 pounds ground beef
6 medium tomatoes, cubed
2 medium green peppers chopped
1 large, or 2 small onions, chopped
4 cloves garlic, minced
1 can (15 1/2 ounces) chili beans, undrained
3 tablespoons chili powder
2 teaspoons salt
1/2 teaspoon ground tumeric
1/2 teaspoon Italian seasoning
1/2 teaspoon ground cumin
1/4 teaspoon cayenne pepper

INSTRUCTIONS
In a large pot, cook beef until no longer pink, then drain. Add tomatoes, green peppers, onions, and garlic. Cook over low to medium low heat, stirring occasionally for 25 to 30 minutes or until vegetables are tender. Add beans and seasonings, mix. Simmer uncovered, for 50 minutes or until thick.

Past Master's Find
(Fried Frog Legs)
Number of servings: 6

INGREDIENTS
12 frog legs
1 cup chopped parsley
1/2 cup lemon juice
1 teaspoon salt
2 eggs
1 cup sifted bread crumbs
Oil for frying
Salt and pepper
Sliced lemons and parsley to garnish
Cajun spice

INSTRUCTIONS
Cook frog legs about 3 minutes in boiling water, containing ½ cup lemon juice and salt. Remove, dry and season with Cajun spice. Dip in a batter made of 2 well-beaten eggs, then roll in bread crumbs. Cover frogs well and drop in oil heated to boiling point. Fry to a golden brown. Remove from oil and drain well. Fry parsley for 1 minute. Lay frog legs on a dish, garnishing with fried parsley and sliced lemon.

Reobligation Banquet
(Spaghetti and Creole Meat Gravy)
Number of servings: 8 - 10

INGREDIENTS

2 pounds ground beef (preferably chuck) or 1 1/2 pounds ground beef and
1/2 pound ground pork
1/3 cup olive oil or vegetable oil
1 large onion, chopped
4 cloves garlic, minced
1 large sweet (green) pepper, chopped
1/2 cup parsley, chopped fine (or 1/2 cup dried)
4 teaspoons salt
1 teaspoon black pepper
1/4 teaspoon (or to taste) cayenne pepper
1/2 teaspoon basil
1/8 teaspoon oregano
1/4 teaspoon paprika
1 small can tomato paste
1 large can (28 ounce) Progresso Italian tomatoes, chopped
1 large can or jar sliced mushrooms
2 tablespoons Worcestershire sauce
1/2 cup red wine (optional)
2 or 3 cups hot water
1/2 cup grated Parmesan cheese
2 lbs of spaghetti

INSTRUCTIONS

Heat oil over medium heat in large iron or heavy pot. Sauté onions, garlic, and sweet pepper until soft. Add meat and continue stirring until lightly browned, slowly adding seasonings as meat and vegetables cook. Next add tomato paste, rinsing can with about 1/4 can water and add to meat. Brown slightly, stirring quickly and well. Add Worcestershire sauce, tomatoes, mushrooms, wine and water. Stir well and the add 1/2 cup Parmesan cheese. Raise heat, bring to a boil, stir well, then lower heat. Partially cover and simmer slowly for about 2 hours. When ready to serve, pour over cooked spaghetti, topping liberally with Parmesan cheese. This recipe will cover 2 pounds of spaghetti. If cooking less spaghetti, remainder of sauce freezes well.

Desserts

Treasurer's Delight
(Lemon Ice Dessert)
Number of servings: 6

INGREDIENTS
2 cups graham cracker crumbs
1/4 cup margarine
1/2 gallon low fat or regular vanilla ice cream
6 ounce can frozen lemonade
6 x 8 inch square pan

INSTRUCTIONS
Take 3 tablespoons of graham cracker crumbs and reserve them on the side. Melt the margarine and combine it with the remaining graham cracker crumbs. Press the crumbs into the bottom and sides of an approximately 9 x 8 inch square pan to make a graham cracker crust. Leave out ice cream until it softens, then mix together thoroughly with the can of lemonade. Spread into the pan evenly and lightly sprinkle the top with the reserve graham cracker crumbs. Refrigerate a few hours until it is frozen, then serve.

E.A. Treat
(Fruit Cake Cookies)
Number of servings: about 16 cookies

INGREDIENTS
1/2 cup butter
1 cup brown sugar
4 eggs
3 teaspoons baking soda
2 cups flour
1 1/2 pounds pecans (6 cups)
1 pound candied cherries
1/2 pound candied pineapple
3 boxes dated
1/4 cup blackberry wine

INSTRUCTIONS
Preheat oven to 250 degrees and grease cookie sheet. Let butter soften, then cream together butter, brown sugar and eggs. Gradually add in baking soda and flour. Blend well. Break pecans into halves and add in pecans, cherries, pineapple, and dates. Lastly add and mix in Blackberry wine. Drop by teaspoonful on cookie sheet, baking about twenty minutes or until lightly browned. Careful not to overcook.

Upright Dessert
(Tuit Suite Apple Pie)
Number of servings: 6

INGREDIENTS
Pillsbury all-ready Pie Crusts (2 crusts) or pie crust of your choice
6 cups thinly sliced, pared tart apples (about 5 or 6 cups)
2/3 cup of sugar
1/2 teaspoon salt
2 tablespoons flour
1 teaspoon cinnamon
1/4 teaspoon nutmeg
1 tablespoon lemon juice
2 tablespoon butter

INSTRUCTIONS
Prepare pie crust according to package directions. Combine apples and rest of ingredients except butter. Put into shell, dot with butter. Cover with remaining shell, tucking edges under and fluting edges, cut 4 slits in top. Bake at 400 degrees for 55 minutes. Cool on rack. Serve with whipped cream or ice cream.

Light of the Meal
(Banana Swirl)
Number of servings: 4

INGREDIENTS
3 egg whites
1/2 pint whipping cream
Pinch of salt
4 large, ripe bananas
1/4 teaspoon cream of tartar
3/4 cup of sugar

INSTRUCTIONS
Separate egg whites and let them warm to room temperature. Beat egg whites and salt with an electric mixer until frothy. Add cream of tartar and continue beating until stiff. Add sugar in four portions and beat well after each addition. Separate mixture lightly over sides and bottom of well-greased pie pan. Bake at low heat in oven, about 225 degrees, for 1 1/2 hours. If your oven does not register lower than 250 degrees, leave the door slightly ajar. This meringue should be a pale cream color. Remove from oven and cool. Loosen gently from pan. Slice bananas into shell and cover with whipped cream. Strawberries, peaches, or lemon cream may be substituted for bananas.

Fraternal Offering
(Strawberry Treat)
Number of servings: 6

INGREDIENTS
2 pkg. (3 ounces each) strawberry flavored gelatin
1 can (1 pound 4 1/2 ounces) crushed pineapple with juice
1/4 cup sugar
1 banana, mashed
1 cup boiling water
1 cup dairy sour cream
1 pint strawberries, sliced
Strawberries for garnish

INSTRUCTIONS
Mix gelatin and sugar in a bowl. Pour boiling water over gelatin, stirring until dissolved. Blend in strawberries, pineapple, and banana. Chill until partially set. In a chilled bowl with chilled beaters, whip sour cream until double in volume (about 5 minutes with electric mixer on highest speed). Gently beat sour cream into gelatin mixture. Pour into an 8 cup mold. Chill until firm. Unmold onto plate and serve garnished with strawberries.

On the Level Sweets
(Pears Baked in Wine)
Number of servings: 6

INGREDIENTS
6 large pears
2 cups dry wine (Burgundy, Chianti, or Barolo)
1/2 cup of sugar
6 whole cloves
A few drops of red food coloring (optional)

INSTRUCTIONS
Wash pears, but do not remove stems. Choose a dish that just fits the pears when standing upright. Pour the wine over the pears almost to their tops. Sprinkle with sugar, and add the cloves. If using food coloring, stir into wine and mix. Bake at 400 degrees for one hour, or until the pears are tender. Remove pears and place in a serving bowl. Pour the remaining wine into a small pot and boil it down until almost syrupy. Pour over pears and serve either warm or cold.

Plumb Good
(Cream Cheese Ice Cream)
Number of servings: 6

INGREDIENTS
2 pints of Creole cream cheese or
(7 ounces Farmer's cheese or 7 ounces large curd cottage cheese pressed together with 1/2 cup heavy whipping cream poured over either choice)
1 can evaporated milk
1 cup sugar
1 large can crushed pineapple
Juice of half lemon
1/2 to 2/3 water

INSTRUCTIONS
Mix all ingredients, stirring well. Place in rectangular dish or pan and put in freezer. When it is almost hard – about 1 hour – take out and stir well. Place back in freezer. Serve soft or cut into squares with knife.

Fellowcraft Wages
(Carrot Cake)
Number of servings: 6

INGREDIENTS
2 cups all-purpose flour
2 teaspoons baking soda
2 teaspoons baking powder
2 teaspoons cinnamon
1 teaspoon salt
3 eggs
3/4 cup vegetable oil
3/4 cup buttermilk
2 cups sugar
2 teaspoons vanilla extract
1 (8 ounce.) can crushed pineapple, drained
2 cups grated carrots
1/2 cup chopped pecans

Cream Cheese Frosting
1/4 pound margarine, room temperature
1 box (1 pound.) sifted confectioners sugar
1 package (8 ounce) cream cheese, room temperature
1 teaspoon grated orange peel
1 teaspoon orange juice

INSTRUCTIONS

Preheat oven to 350 degrees. Generously Greece two 9 inch pans and set aside. Sift flour, baking soda, cinnamon, and salt together and set aside. In a large bowl, beat eggs. Add oil, buttermilk, sugar, and vanilla and mix well. Add flour mixture, pineapple, carrots, and pecans. Stir well and pour into cake pans. Bake 45 minutes or until pick inserted in center comes out clean. Cool completely and frost cake with cream cheese frosting. Refrigerate until frosting is set. Serve chilled.

Cream Cheese Icing: Cream margarine and cream cheese until fluffy. And vanilla, powdered sugar, orange juice, and orange peel. Beat until of spreading consistency. Spread between and over layers of cake.

Three Steps to Smile
(Bread Pudding)
Number of servings: 6 - 8

INGREDIENTS
4 cups day old French bread, cubed
4 large Granny Smith green apples, or 4 red apples, peeled and shredded
4 eggs, slightly beaten
4 1/2 cups milk, heated
1/2 cup melted butter
1 cup raisins
1 cup sugar
1 teaspoon cinnamon
2 teaspoons vanilla
1/2 teaspoon salt

INSTRUCTIONS
Combine bread and milk in a large bowl and set aside. In a separate bowl beat eggs, add sugar and mix well. Stir into bread mixture, adding apples, vanilla, cinnamon, salt, butter, and raisins. Pour into buttered 2 quarts shallow baking pan. Bake at 350 degrees in preheated oven for one hour or until knife inserted in center comes out clean. If you like more creamy pudding, bake with pan sitting in a pan of warm water about 1 inch deep. Serve plain or with brandy or lemon sauce.

Chaplain's Sin
(Peach Cup)
Number of servings: 6

INGREDIENTS
8 or 9 fresh ripe peached
1/2 teaspoon cinnamon
1 cup sifted flour
1/2 cup butter or margarine
1 cup sugar
1/4 teaspoon salt
Light cream

INSTRUCTIONS
Wash peaches and peel. Slice peaches and place in lightly buttered 8 x 8 x 2 inch baking dish. Sift flour along with sugar, salt, and cinnamon into medium sized bowl. Mix butter until it resembles coarse corn meal. Sprinkle mixture evenly over peaches. Bake 45 to 50 minutes in a preheated 375 degrees oven or until topping is a golden color and peached tender. Serve warm in sherbet dishes with cream.

Working Tool Reward
(Cream Cheese Pie)
Number of servings: 6 - 8

INGREDIENTS
Cream Cheese mixture:
2 small packages (8 ounce) cream cheese
1 egg
1 teaspoon vanilla
1/4 cup sugar
1/4 teaspoon salt
Pecan mixture:
3 eggs
1 teaspoon vanilla
3/4 cup corn syrup
2 tablespoons sugar
1 1/4 cup chopped pecans
1 unbaked pastry shell (9 inch)

INSTRUCTIONS
In one bowl beat together ingredients for cream cheese mixture (cream cheese, egg, vanilla, sugar, and salt). In another bowl, beat 3 eggs until yolk and whites combine. Add sugar, vanilla, and corn syrup. Beat until gently blended. Spread cream cheese mixture to cover the pastry shell. Sprinkle with pecans. Gently pour syrup mixture over pecans. Bake at 375 degrees until center is firm to touch, 35 to 40 mixtures. Bake in low rack in oven.

Lagniappe

Preparing Dried Beans for Cooking

INSTRUCTIONS

Packaged dried beans should be rinsed under cold running water, discarding broken or defective beans. Dried beans should beans should be soaked before cooking. There are two methods.

For the old fashion method, measure beans in a cup measure and place in a deep pot. Add three cups water for each cup of beans. Soak overnight. If possible, use the nutritious soaking water for cooking beans.

For a quick method, measure beans in a cup measure and place in a deep pot. Add three cups water for each cup of beans. Bring to the boiling point and boil for 2 minutes. Remove from heat, cover pot and let stand at room temperature for one to two hours.

Then proceed to cook beans according to your recipe. Cover slightly beans when cooking. Do not cook beans quickly or over high heat because this breaks their skin. Simmer over low heat, being careful not to overcook. Salt slows their cooking because it toughens them. Acids like wine or tomatoes also slow down the softening process. Add them only when the beans are almost cooked. Beans freeze well.

This method can be used for any type of dried beans.

The Roux

INSTRUCTIONS

To the Creole cook this is the foundation and success of many fine dishes. In making a brown roux, equal parts of flour and butter or flour and oil are used. Never let the roux become over-browned or burnt. It has always been the customary to make the roux in a heavy pot. Slowly heat the oil or butter and gradually add the flour, stirring constantly until it is a golden or dark brown, the color carrying according to the particular dish you are preparing. This is a slow process, taking about 20 minutes to a half hour. The key lies in the gradual introduction of ingredients (which vary according to the individual recipe). This begins the cooking of the desired dish. When adding water to the roux, be sure the water is hot or it will separate the oil and flour.

A white roux is made by blending butter and flour together and slowly adding hot milk. You must never allow a white roux to brown. It is easiest to make a white roux a double boiler. Do not let the water boil beneath your sauce. Keep it at a simmer. Also, the water must not touch the bottom of the upper pan of the double boiler.

Cajun Seasoning

INGREDIENTS

2 tablespoons celery salt

2 tablespoons onion salt

2 tablespoons garlic salt

2 tablespoons paprika

1 teaspoon chili powder

1/4 teaspoon white pepper

1/4 teaspoon black pepper

1/8 teaspoon cayenne pepper

INSTRUCTIONS

Sift all ingredients together several times. Put in empty spice bottle with shaker insert.

Chicken Cooked in Microwave

INGREDIENTS
2 to 3 pound chicken, cut up
1/2 onion, sliced
1 rib celery and leaves, cut into pieces
1 1/2 teaspoons salt
1/2 teaspoon cayenne pepper
1/2 cup dry Vermouth or Satuerne wine
2 cups hot water

INSTRUCTIONS
Place chicken and rest of ingredients in a large, covered, microwave safe, three to five quart casserole. Cook on high for 25 minutes. After cooked, marinate in stock in refrigerator until cool, or overnight. Remove chicken, strain and discard vegetables, and reserve stock. Bone chicken and cut into bite size pieces. Both chicken and stock can be frozen for future use and used for Jambalaya, Gumbo, or any recipe calling for cooked chicken.

More Masonic Books from Cornerstone

Masonic Enlightenment
The Philosophy, History and Wisdom of Freemasonry
Edited by Michael R. Poll
6 x 9 Softcover 180 pages
ISBN 1-887560-75-0

Morgan: The Scandal That Shook Freemasonry
by Stephen Dafoe
Foreword by Arturo de Hoyos
6x9 Softcover 484 pages
ISBN 1-934935-54-9

Masonic Questions and Answers
by Paul M. Bessel
6 x 9 Softcover 144 pages
ISBN 1-887560-59-9

Our Stations and Places - Masonic Officer's Handbook
by Henry G. Meacham
Revised by Michael R. Poll
6 x 9 Softcover 164 pages
ISBN: 1-887560-63-7

Knights & Freemasons: The Birth of Modern Freemasonry
By Albert Pike & Albert Mackey
Edited by Michael R. Poll
Foreword by S. Brent Morris
6 x 9 Softcover 178 pages
ISBN 1-887560-66-1

Robert's Rules of Order: Masonic Edition
Revised by Michael R. Poll
6 x 9 Softcover 212 pages
ISBN 1-887560-07-6

Cornerstone Book Publishers
www.cornerstonepublishers.com

More Masonic Books from Cornerstone

Historical Inquiry into the Origins of the Ancient and Accepted Scottish Rite
by James Foulhouze
Foreword by Michael R. Poll
6x9 Softcover 216 pages
ISBN 1-613420-26-9

A General History of Freemasonry
by Emmanuel Rebold
Translated by J. Fletcher Brennan
Softcover 434 pages
ISBN 1-934935-81-6

Lectures of the Ancient and Primitive Rite of Freemasonry
by John Yarker
6x9 Softcover 218 pages
ISBN 1-934935-10-7

The Schism Between the Scotch & York Rites
by Charles Laffon de Ladébat
6x9 Softcover 66 pages
ISBN 1-934935-33-6

The Ceremony of Initiation
by W.L. Wilmshurst
6x9 Softcover 74 pages
ISBN 1-934935-02-6

The Master Workman or True Masonic Guide
by Henry C. Atwood
6x9 Softcover 396 pages
ISBN 1613420528

Cornerstone Book Publishers
www.cornerstonepublishers.com

www.ingramcontent.com/pod-product-compliance
Lightning Source LLC
Chambersburg PA
CBHW032026090426
42741CB00006B/749